Level 1
Second Edition
Assessment/Resource Booklet

Authors
Matthew Stephens
Hope Tolbert

Teacher
Matthew Stephens

Senior Consultant
Mary McGee

Designer
Boston Stephens

Project Coordinator
Athena Lester

Editors
Athena Lester
Danielle Nettleton

417-256-4191
www.essentialsinwriting.com
Copyright © 2019 by Matthew B. Stephens

Printed in the United States of America
Update December 2020

Assessments

Assessment 1 – Letters, Words, & Sentences; Spacing Words; and Capitalizing Sentences (Lessons 2-4)

A. Rewrite the following sentences with *spaces* between words.

1. Thebedis old.

_____

2. Samcan sing.

_____

3. Dogs arefuzzy.

_____

B. Rewrite each sentence below and *capitalize* the first word.

1. kat jumps.

_____

2. the fox rests.

_____

3. i jumped in the water.

_____

4. the tram stops.

_____

ASSESSMENT

Assessment 2 – Sentence Subjects and Sentence Predicates (Lessons 5-6)

A. Underline the *subject* of each sentence.

1. The child sang a song.

2. The panda snacks on the twigs.

3. Sal picked the bud.

4. Mom went to the pond.

B. Underline the *predicate* of each sentence.

1. The bunny hopped.

2. Cal tosses the ball.

3. The girl ran up the hill.

4. The frog jumped in the pond.

C. Fill in each blank with one of the following *subjects*.

My sister	The small kitten	The truck

1. _____ sped up the path.

2. _____ sang a song.

3. _____ lapped the milk.

D. Fill in each blank with one of the following *predicates*.

sniffs	has fins	is Ted

1. The dog _____.

2. My brother _____.

3. The fish _____.

ASSESSMENT

E. Complete each sentence with a *subject* or a *predicate*.

1. A puppy _____.

2. _____ called his dad.

3. The robber _____.

4. _____ bangs the drums.

5. _____ washes the truck.

F. Underline the *subjects* and circle the *predicates* in the following sentences.

1. The vet helped the pet.
2. The red robin sang.
3. Jon kicks the ball.
4. I lost a penny.
5. The woman walked to the hill.

G. Complete the sentences with a *subject* or a *predicate*.

1. _____ ran back.

2. The black cat _____.

3. _____ dropped his hat.

4. The small kid _____.

Assessment 3 – Complete and Incomplete Sentences (Lessons 7-8)

● **A. Rewrite the *incomplete sentences* and change them into *complete sentences* on the lines provided.**

1. The tall girl.

_____

2. Ran fast.

_____

3. Went to the path.

_____

4. The fuzzy duck.

_____

● **B. The sentences below are *incomplete*. Write "S" if the sentences are missing a *subject* and "P" if they are missing a *predicate*.**

1. The glad woman.   **What is missing?**   _____

2. Kissed the frog.   **What is missing?**   _____

3. The sad swan.   **What is missing?**   _____

4. Ben.   **What is missing?**   _____

5. Ran up the hill.   **What is missing?**   _____

C. Finish the *incomplete sentences* on the lines below.

1. The big dog _____.

2. _____ sat on a log.

3. Jen and Kim _____.

● 4. _____ went to bed.

ASSESSMENT

Assessment 4 – Declarative, Interrogative, Exclamatory, and Imperative Sentences (Lessons 9-12)

A. Rewrite the *declarative sentence* below so it ends with a period.

Pandas are big

_____

B. On the line below, write a *declarative sentence.*

_____

C. Rewrite the *interrogative sentence* below so it ends with a question mark.

Are you from Kansas

_____

D. On the line below, write an *interrogative sentence.*

_____

E. Rewrite the *exclamatory sentence* below so it ends with an exclamation point.

My sister is the best

_____

F. On the line below, write an *exclamatory sentence.*

_____

G. Rewrite the *imperative sentence* so it ends with a period or exclamation point.

Wash the glass

_____

H. On the line below, write an *imperative sentence.*

_____

ASSESSMENT

Assessment 5 – Practice Writing Sentences (Lesson 13)

A. Write whether each sentence is _declarative, interrogative, exclamatory,_ **or** _imperative._

1. Are you in class?   _____

2. The fox digs.   _____

3. Toss the trash.   _____

4. This is fun!   _____

B. Write sentences according the instructions below.

1. Write an **imperative sentence** about **a dog.**

_____

2. Write an **exclamatory sentence** about **a truck.**

_____

3. Write a **declarative sentence** about **a dress.**

_____

4. Write an **interrogative sentence** about **a hat.**

_____

C. The sentences below have mistakes in capitalization and punctuation. Rewrite the sentences correctly.

1. the man went to Texas

_____

2. where is my sister

_____

ASSESSMENT

Assessment 6 – Common and Proper Nouns (Lessons 14-16)

A. Underline all *common nouns* in the sentences below.

1. The fox digs a den.

2. The boy held the box.

3. The man dropped the letter.

4. The bunny sniffed the grass.

5. The woman runs.

B. Underline all *proper nouns* in the sentences below.

1. Beck hid the lock.

2. Dan went to Kansas.

3. Ben and Pat are brothers.

4. Sid bangs the drums.

5. Mal went to Alaska.

C. Underline all *nouns* in the sentences below.

1. Lin talks to Ken.

2. The boys went to class.

3. Sid swims in the pond.

4. Jon walks on the path.

5. Pandas live in China.

ASSESSMENT

Assessment 7 – Singular and Plural Nouns (Lesson 17)

A. Underline all *singular nouns* in the sentences below.

1. The boy is small.

2. Grab a pen!

3. The woman is tall.

4. Put away the toys.

5. A panda is black and white.

B. Underline all *plural nouns* in the sentences below.

1. Meg kissed her dolls.

2. Grandpa has three cars.

3. The mats are green.

4. The bags are full.

5. A tree is big.

C. Fill in the blank with the *plural* of the indicated noun.

1. Fran saw _____ at the mall. (*cat*)

2. The _____ were on a sled. (*girl*)

3. Mom got two _____. (*rug*)

4. The _____ fell down the steps! (*box*)

ASSESSMENT

Assessment 8 – Adjectives (Lesson 18)

A. Underline each _adjective_ in the sentences below.

1. I strummed the sad song.

2. Jeb has black shoes.

3. The woman jumped in the cold water.

B. Complete each sentence below with your own _adjective_.

1. Tim picked the _____ candy.

2. Willa had a _____ belt.

3. The _____ boy hopped.

4. Cam has a _____ brother.

C. Rewrite each sentence below and add your own _adjective_.

1. Claire walked to the bench.

_____

2. The dog sniffed.

_____

3. The man washes the truck.

_____

4. The rabbit hops.

_____

5. The glass fell.

_____

ASSESSMENT

Assessment 9 – Action Verbs (Lesson 19)

● **A. Underline each *action verb* in the sentences below.**

1. Jen lifts the box.

2. The buck drinks.

3. The man drops the dish.

4. Liv dances.

5. Ash swims.

B. Complete each sentence below with your own *action verb*.

1. The rabbit _____.

2. Will _____ in the attic.

● 3. The rat _____ the apple.

4. The girl _____ to the hill.

C. Fill in each blank with the correct *action verb*.

swims	run	sniffs	kicked

1. The fish _____ in the pond.

2. The puppy _____ the boy.

3. Ted _____ the soccer ball.

● 4. The kids _____ by the fence.

ASSESSMENT

Assessment 10 – Nouns, Adjectives, and Action Verbs (Lesson 20)

Find and underline the *nouns*, circle the *adjectives*, and draw a box around the *action verbs* in each line below.

1.	cat	jump	Jen	vest
2.	sang	bird	swim	hot
3.	child	ran	Kansas	happy
4.	pink	desk	glad	said
5.	box	fluffy	tell	sit
6.	called	pug	red	panda
7.	belt	odd	tells	soft
8.	gives	Ann	tall	picked
9.	rabbit	ended	India	cold
10.	old	woman	long	sniffs

ASSESSMENT

Unit One Comprehensive Assessment (Lessons 2-20)

Circle the letter next to the correct answer.

1. *The puppy bit the snack.*

   Which of the following is the *subject* of this sentence?

   A. snack

   B. The puppy

   C. bit

   D. the snack

2. *The girl sends a letter.*

   Which of the following is the *predicate* of this sentence?

   A. The girl

   B. girl

   C. letter

   D. sends a letter

3. Which sentence is *incomplete*?

   A. The kid jumps.

   B. Sings the song.

   C. The women dance.

   D. Elle runs.

4. Which of the following words is a *noun*?

   A. hill

   B. walked

   C. happy

   D. melted

5. Which of the following words is a *proper noun*?

   A. leg

   B. Kansas

   C. fox

   D. bends

6. Which of the following is a *plural noun*?

    A. pug

    B. net

    C. beds

    D. fin

7. *The sad boy walked.*

    Which of the following is the *adjective* in this sentence?

    A. The

    B. sad

    C. boy

    D. walked

8. *The bunny nibbled the long grass.*

    Which of the following is the *action verb* in this sentence?

    A. bunny

    B. nibbled

    C. long

    D. grass

9. An *interrogative sentence* ends with a _____.

    A. period

    B. question mark

    C. exclamation point

    D. period or exclamation point

10. *Wash the dishes.*

    What kind of sentence is this?

    A. declarative

    B. interrogative

    C. exclamatory

    D. imperative

Assessment 11 – List of Items & Paragraphs (Lessons 22-31)

Circle the letter next to the correct answer.

1. Which item does *not* belong in a list of animals?

   A. pigs

   B. dogs

   C. socks

   D. cats

2. What is the correct order of the parts of a paragraph?

   A. Closing Sentence, Indent, Body Sentences, Opening Sentence

   B. Opening Sentence, Indent, Closing Sentence, Body Sentences

   C. Indent, Opening Sentence, Body Sentences, Closing Sentence

   D. Indent, Body Sentences, Opening Sentence, Closing Sentence

3. Which sentence does *not* belong in a paragraph about summer?

   A. My family swims in the summer.

   B. I went sledding.

   C. I went to the beach.

   D. It is hot.

Read the following paragraph body:

They make nests. Robins lay eggs. They sing songs! Robins are neat.

4. Choose the *best* opening sentence for the paragraph above.

   A. Robins are cool birds.

   B. My sister has long hair.

   C. I have a dog.

   D. They have wings.

Assessment 11 – Paragraph

Write a paragraph about your favorite food.

1. ***Indent*** the first sentence in your paragraph by leaving a space in front of it. You may use your finger to make the space.

2. Write an ***opening sentence*** to introduce your topic.

3. Write at least three ***body sentences*** that tell your reader about your topic.

4. ***Stay on topic!*** Do not include sentences that are not about your topic.

5. Finish your paragraph by writing a ***closing sentence.***

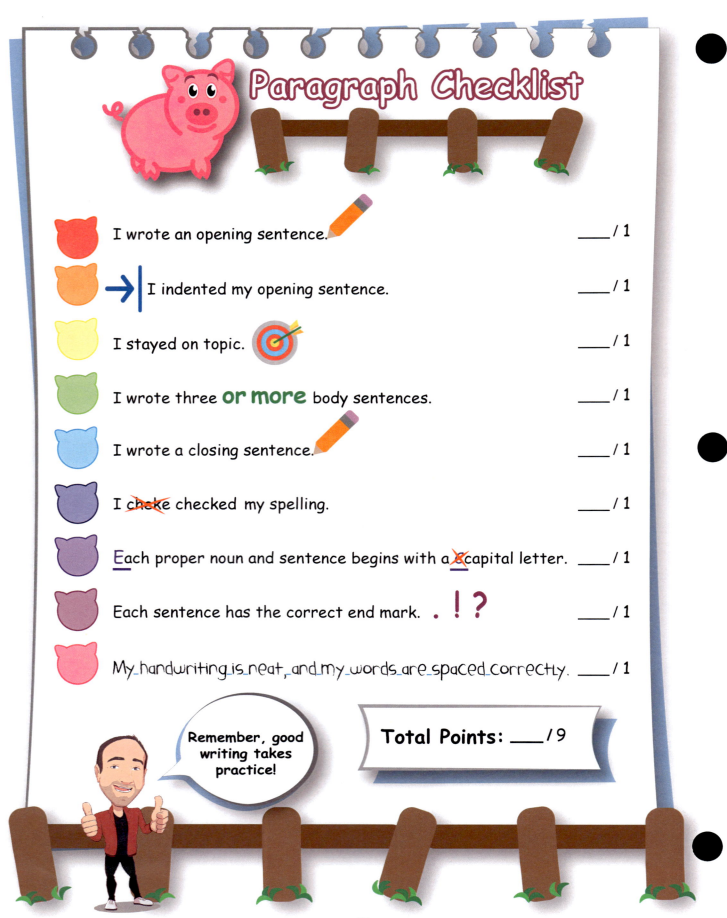

Paragraph Checklist

I wrote an opening sentence. ___ / 1

→| I indented my opening sentence. ___ / 1

I stayed on topic. ___ / 1

I wrote three **or more** body sentences. ___ / 1

I wrote a closing sentence. ___ / 1

I ~~cheke~~ checked my spelling. ___ / 1

Each proper noun and sentence begins with a ~~X~~ capital letter. ___ / 1

Each sentence has the correct end mark. **. ! ?** ___ / 1

My handwriting is neat, and my words are spaced correctly. ___ / 1

Remember, good writing takes practice!

Total Points: ___ / 9

Assessment 12 – Personal Letter (Lessons 32-34)

A. Read the _letter_ below and label its parts in the correct boxes.

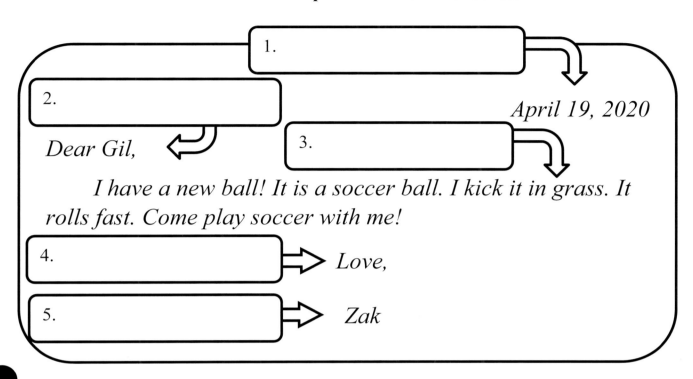

1.

2.

Dear Gil,

3.

April 19, 2020

I have a new ball! It is a soccer ball. I kick it in grass. It rolls fast. Come play soccer with me!

4.

Love,

5.

Zak

B. Write the correct dates on the lines provided below. Remember to write the month, day, year, and a comma.

1. Today

_____

2. Yesterday

_____

3. Tomorrow

_____

4. The day after tomorrow

_____

5. Christmas this year

_____

ASSESSMENT

Assessment 12 – Personal Letter

Write a letter to your friend telling them about your family.

 1. Write the **date** on the right side of your paper.

 2. Write the **greeting** on the left side of your paper on the second line.

 3. Write a **body** paragraph. Be sure to indent and stay on topic. Read your body paragraph to look for mistakes.

 4. Create a **closing** after the body. Begin your closing in the middle of the next line.

 5. End your letter with your **signature.** Write your name on the last line under the closing.

Personal Letter Checklist

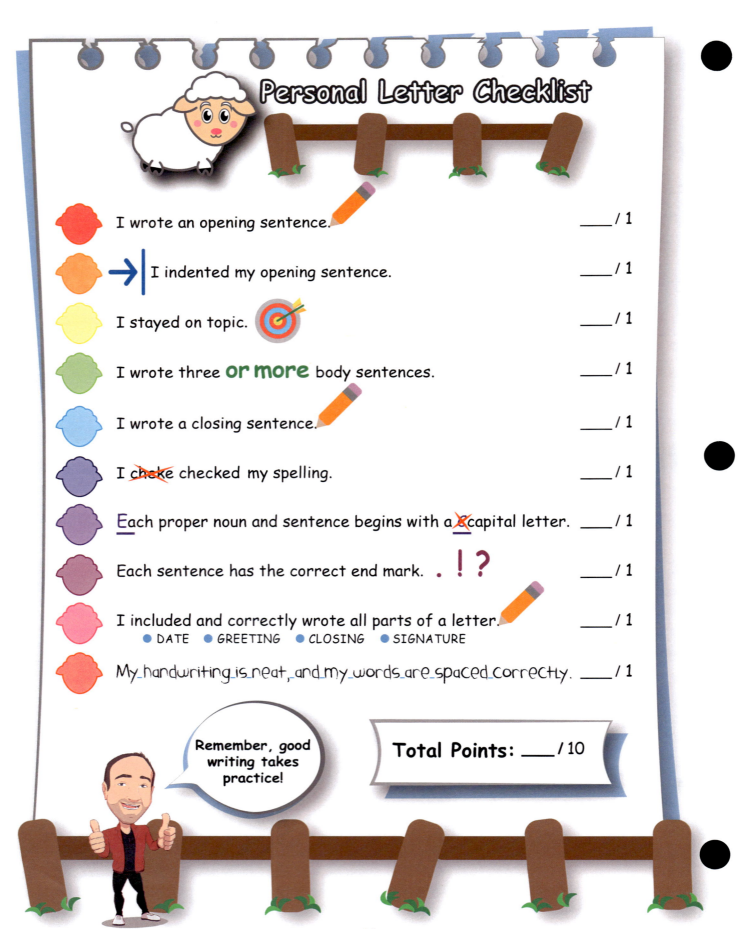

I wrote an opening sentence. ___ / 1

I indented my opening sentence. ___ / 1

I stayed on topic. ___ / 1

I wrote three **or more** body sentences. ___ / 1

I wrote a closing sentence. ___ / 1

I ~~cheke~~ checked my spelling. ___ / 1

Each proper noun and sentence begins with a ~~x~~ capital letter. ___ / 1

Each sentence has the correct end mark. . ! ? ___ / 1

I included and correctly wrote all parts of a letter. ___ / 1
● DATE   ● GREETING   ● CLOSING   ● SIGNATURE

My handwriting is neat, and my words are spaced correctly. ___ / 1

Remember, good writing takes practice!

Total Points: ___/ 10

Assessment 13 – Personal Narrative (Lessons 35-38)

A. The events below are not in *order*. Number the events in the *order* that they happened. Pay attention to *transitions*.

1. _____ Next, I grabbed a pen.

   _____ Finally, I wrote the letter.

   _____ First, I sat at the desk.

2. _____ Finally, I spotted him at the park.

   _____ First, I led my dog on a walk.

   _____ Then, he ran off.

   _____ Next, the leash snapped.

   _____ He was lost!

3. _____ First, I got in my truck.

   _____ Finally, I saw the pandas.

   _____ Next, I went to the zoo.

4. _____ Next, I got my sled.

   _____ First, snow fell.

   _____ I went down the hill.

   _____ Then, I walked up the hill.

   _____ Finally, I headed home.

5. _____ I played at the park.

   _____ Then, I walked to the park.

   _____ First, I got up.

   _____ Finally, I went home.

   _____ Next, I got dressed.

ASSESSMENT

Assessment 13 – Personal Narrative

Write a personal narrative about your birthday.

 1. ***Indent*** the first sentence in your personal narrative by leaving a space in front of it. You may use your finger to make the space.

 2. Write an ***opening sentence*** to introduce your personal narrative.

 3. Write at least four ***events*** in the order that they happened.

 4. Use ***transitions!*** Use words like "first," "then," and "next" to show order.

 5. Finish your personal narrative by writing a ***closing sentence.***

Personal Narrative Checklist

I indented my opening sentence. ___/ 1

My opening sentence grabs my reader's attention. ___/ 1

I wrote at least four events. ___/ 1

I used at least three transitions. ___/ 1

I stayed on topic. ___/ 1

I wrote a closing sentence. ___/ 1

I ~~choke~~ checked my spelling. ___/ 1

Each proper noun and sentence begins with a capital letter. ___/ 1

Each sentence has the correct end mark. . ! ? ___/ 1

My handwriting is neat, and my words are spaced correctly. ___/ 1

Remember, good writing takes practice!

Total Points: ___/ 10

Assessment 14 – Imaginative Narrative (Lessons 39-42)

A. The events below are not in *order*. Number the events in the *order* that they happened. Pay attention to *transitions*.

1. _____ Next, it went to the fridge.

   _____ First, a skunk walked in.

   _____ The skunk had lunch!

2. _____ Then, he flew.

   _____ Next, he grew wings.

   _____ First, the cat jumped off the steps.

3. _____ Finally, the pug ran off.

   _____ First, Max sketched a pug.

   _____ Then, Max talked to the pug.

   _____ Next, the pug was alive!

   _____ They were friends.

4. _____ First, Mel got a boat.

   _____ Finally, she landed in the sand.

   _____ Next, she drifted on the water.

5. _____ First, the bunny hopped on a bus.

   _____ Next, he went to Kansas.

   _____ Finally, he went home.

   _____ Then, he went to Texas!

   _____ He liked to travel.

ASSESSMENT

Assessment 14 – Imaginative Narrative

> *Write a narrative about a trip to the moon.*

 1. ***Indent*** the first sentence in your narrative by leaving a space in front of it. You may use your finger to make the space.

 2. Write an ***opening sentence*** to introduce your narrative.

 3. Write at least four ***events*** in the order that they happened.

 4. Use ***transitions!*** Use words like "first," "then," and "next" to show order.

 5. Finish your narrative by writing a ***closing sentence.***

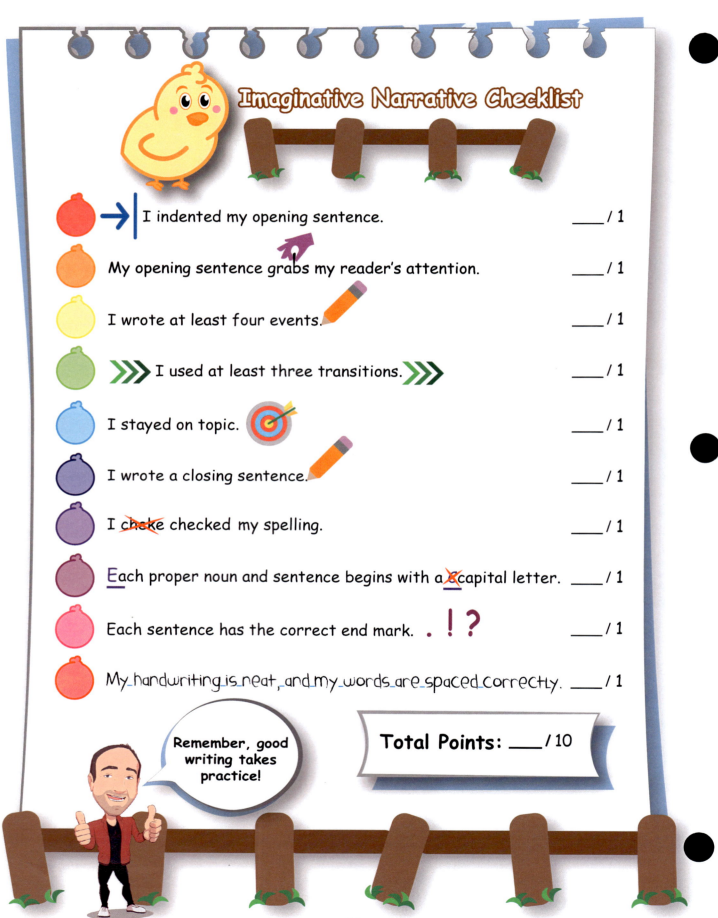

Imaginative Narrative Checklist

I indented my opening sentence.   ___ / 1

My opening sentence grabs my reader's attention.   ___ / 1

I wrote at least four events.   ___ / 1

I used at least three transitions.   ___ / 1

I stayed on topic.   ___ / 1

I wrote a closing sentence.   ___ / 1

I ~~choke~~ checked my spelling.   ___ / 1

Each proper noun and sentence begins with a ~~x~~capital letter.   ___ / 1

Each sentence has the correct end mark. . ! ?   ___ / 1

My handwriting is neat, and my words are spaced correctly.   ___ / 1

Remember, good writing takes practice!

Total Points: ___ / 10

Unit Two Comprehensive Assessment (Lessons 22-42)

Circle the letter next to the correct answer.

1. What is the correct order of the parts of a paragraph?

    A. Opening Sentence, Body Sentences, Indent, Closing Sentence

    B. Closing Sentence, Indent, Body Sentences, Opening Sentence

    C. Indent, Opening Sentence, Body Sentences, Closing Sentence

    D. Body Sentences, Closing Sentence, Opening Sentence, Indent

Read the following paragraph body:

They live in swamps. Frogs have spots. They jump. Frogs are fun.

2. Choose the best *opening sentence* for the paragraph above.

    A. Cats are fuzzy.

    B. I went to the zoo.

    C. Swamps are big.

    D. Frogs are neat.

3. Which part of the *paragraph* introduces your topic?

    A. Indent

    B. Opening Sentence

    C. Body Sentences

    D. Closing Sentence

4. Which part of the *paragraph* is the small space you leave before the first sentence?

    A. Indent

    B. Opening Sentence

    C. Body Sentences

    D. Closing Sentence

5. Which of the following does not belong in a *paragraph* about rabbits?

    A. They munch grass.

    B. They have strong legs.

    C. I swam in the pond.

    D. Rabbits are soft.

6. What is the first part of a *personal letter*?

    A. Body

    B. Date

    C. Signature

    D. Greeting

7. Which *date* is written correctly?

    A. May 5, 1999

    B. 5 1999, May

    C. 1999 May 5

    D. May 5 1999

8. Which of the following events would come first in a *personal narrative*?

    A. Next, I saw a lion.

    B. First, I went to the zoo.

    C. He roared!

    D. Finally, I ran away.

9. Which of the following events would come last in a *personal narrative*?

    A. Next, I saw a lion.

    B. First, I went to the zoo.

    C. He roared!

    D. Finally, I ran away.

10. _____ help show the order of events in a *narrative*.

    A. Question marks

    B. Transitions

    C. Nouns

    D. Adjectives

Resources

Aa

about	across
again	almost
already	also
always	and
animal	another
any	anyone
are	around
asked	aunt

Bb

babies	baby
balloon	bear
beautiful	because
been	before
believe	black
blow	blue
bought	brother
brown	buy
by	

_____

_____

_____

_____

_____

_____

_____

_____

_____

_____

_____

Cc

call

change

choose

Christmas

clothes

color

coming

cousin

can't

children

chose

climb

cold

come

could

cry

45

Dd

decide	didn't
different	do
doctor	does
doesn't	done
don't	draw
drop	

Ee

early	earth
easy	eight
enough	even
ever	every
everything	except
excited	eye

Ff

family	father
favorite	February
finally	first
follow	forty
found	four
fourth	Friday
friend	from

Gg

get

give

good

grandpa

guess

gift

goes

grandma

great

guest

Hh

half	happened
have	hear
heard	heart
here	honey
hope	horse
hour	house

Ii

ice cream	if
I'll	insect
inside	instead
interesting	into
is	isn't
it	

Jj

jiggle

jump

joke

just

Kk

key   keyboard

kind   king

knew   knock

know

L

ladder	later
laugh	learn
let's	letter
light	like
listen	little
look	loose
lose	love

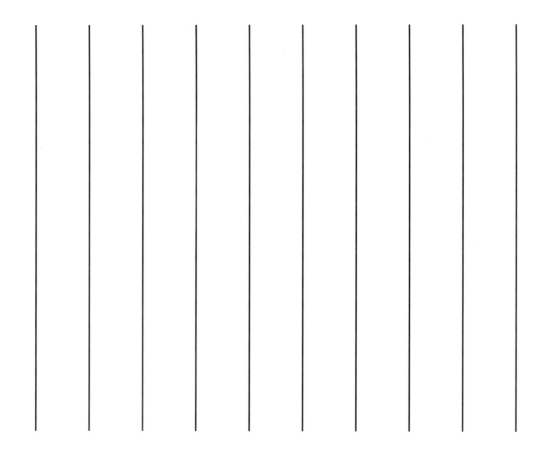

Mm

many   maybe

might   milk

minute   Monday

money   more

morning   mother

mouse   move

my   myself

Nn

neighbor	never
new	next
nice	night
nine	ninety
ninth	none
nothing	now
nurse	

Oo

obey	of
off	often
once	one
only	open
opposite	orange
our	

Pp

party	people
perfect	person
picture	piece
pink	please
point	practice
probably	purple
put	

Qq

quack

queen

quiet

quit

quarter

quick

quilt

quiz

Rr

read

ready

really

reason

remember

right

ring

roar

rough

Ss

safe

said

Saturday

says

school

should

sister

some

something

sometimes

special

Sunday

sure

surprise

Tt

the	their
there	they
thought	threw
through	Thursday
tickle	today
together	tomorrow
tonight	tough
Tuesday	two

Uu

umbrella	until
upon	us
use	used
usual	usually

vacation

very

Ww

want   was

wear   weather

Wednesday   weird

went   were

what   when

where   white

who   with

won't   work

world   would

Write

x-ray

xylophone

yellow

yesterday

you

your

zebra

zero

RESOURCES

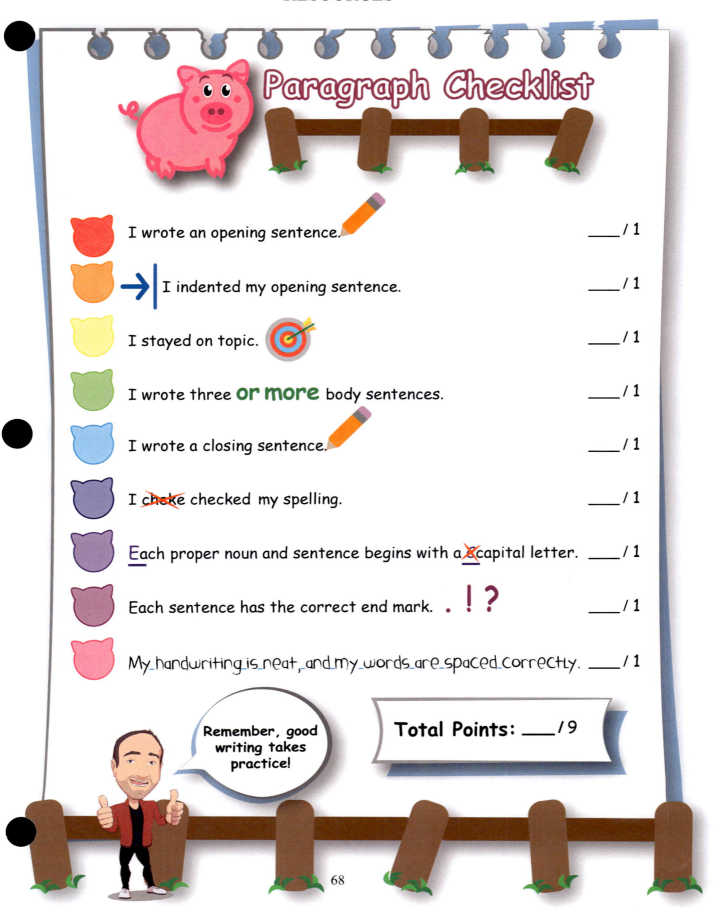

Paragraph Checklist

I wrote an opening sentence. ___ / 1

→| I indented my opening sentence. ___ / 1

I stayed on topic. ___ / 1

I wrote three **or more** body sentences. ___ / 1

I wrote a closing sentence. ___ / 1

I ~~cheke~~ checked my spelling. ___ / 1

Each proper noun and sentence begins with a ~~x~~ capital letter. ___ / 1

Each sentence has the correct end mark. . ! ? ___ / 1

My handwriting is neat, and my words are spaced correctly. ___ / 1

Remember, good writing takes practice!

Total Points: ___ / 9

RESOURCES

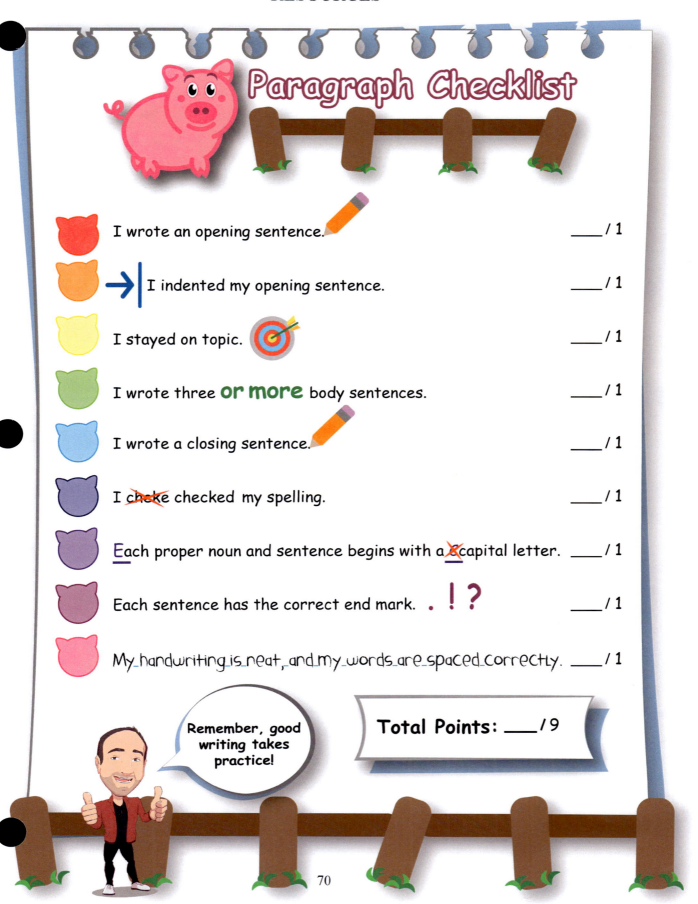

Paragraph Checklist

I wrote an opening sentence.   ___ / 1

➔| I indented my opening sentence.   ___ / 1

I stayed on topic.   ___ / 1

I wrote three **or more** body sentences.   ___ / 1

I wrote a closing sentence.   ___ / 1

I cheke checked my spelling.   ___ / 1

Each proper noun and sentence begins with a capital letter.   ___ / 1

Each sentence has the correct end mark.   . ! ?   ___ / 1

My handwriting is neat, and my words are spaced correctly.   ___ / 1

Remember, good writing takes practice!

Total Points: ___ / 9

RESOURCES

Paragraph Checklist

I wrote an opening sentence. ___/1

→ I indented my opening sentence. ___/1

I stayed on topic. ___/1

I wrote three **or more** body sentences. ___/1

I wrote a closing sentence. ___/1

I ~~cheke~~ checked my spelling. ___/1

Each proper noun and sentence begins with a ~~x~~ capital letter. ___/1

Each sentence has the correct end mark. . ! ? ___/1

My handwriting is neat, and my words are spaced correctly. ___/1

Remember, good writing takes practice!

Total Points: ___/9

RESOURCES

Personal Letter Checklist

I wrote an opening sentence. ___ / 1

I indented my opening sentence. ___ / 1

I stayed on topic. ___ / 1

I wrote three **or more** body sentences. ___ / 1

I wrote a closing sentence. ___ / 1

I cheke checked my spelling. ___ / 1

Each proper noun and sentence begins with a capital letter. ___ / 1

Each sentence has the correct end mark. . ! ? ___ / 1

I included and correctly wrote all parts of a letter. ___ / 1
● DATE   ● GREETING   ● CLOSING   ● SIGNATURE

My handwriting is neat, and my words are spaced correctly. ___ / 1

Remember, good writing takes practice!

Total Points: ___ / 10

RESOURCES

Personal Narrative
Graphic Organizer

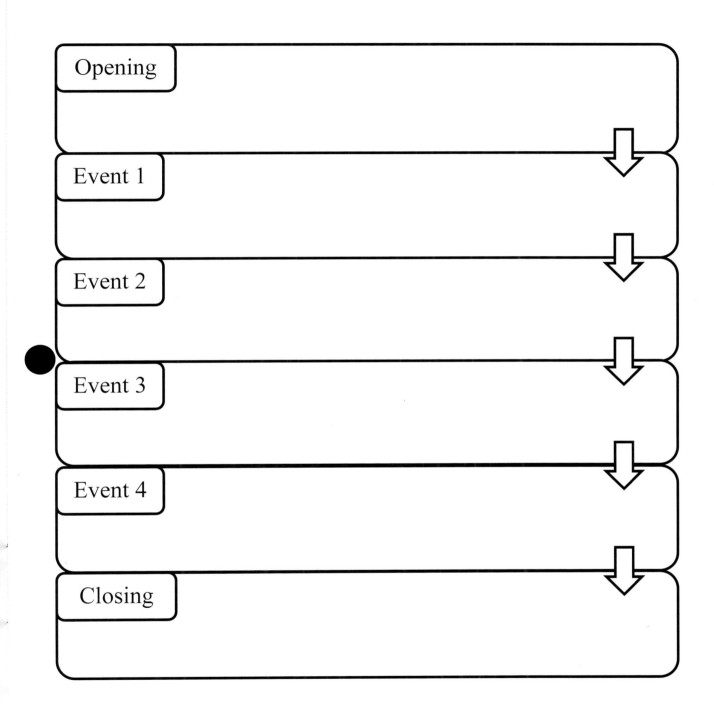

Opening

Event 1

Event 2

Event 3

Event 4

Closing

Personal Narrative Checklist

I indented my opening sentence. ___ / 1

My opening sentence grabs my reader's attention. ___ / 1

I wrote at least four events. ___ / 1

I used at least three transitions. ___ / 1

I stayed on topic. ___ / 1

I wrote a closing sentence. ___ / 1

I choke checked my spelling. ___ / 1

Each proper noun and sentence begins with a capital letter. ___ / 1

Each sentence has the correct end mark. . ! ? ___ / 1

My handwriting is neat, and my words are spaced correctly. ___ / 1

Remember, good writing takes practice!

Total Points: ___ / 10

Imaginative Narrative
Graphic Organizer

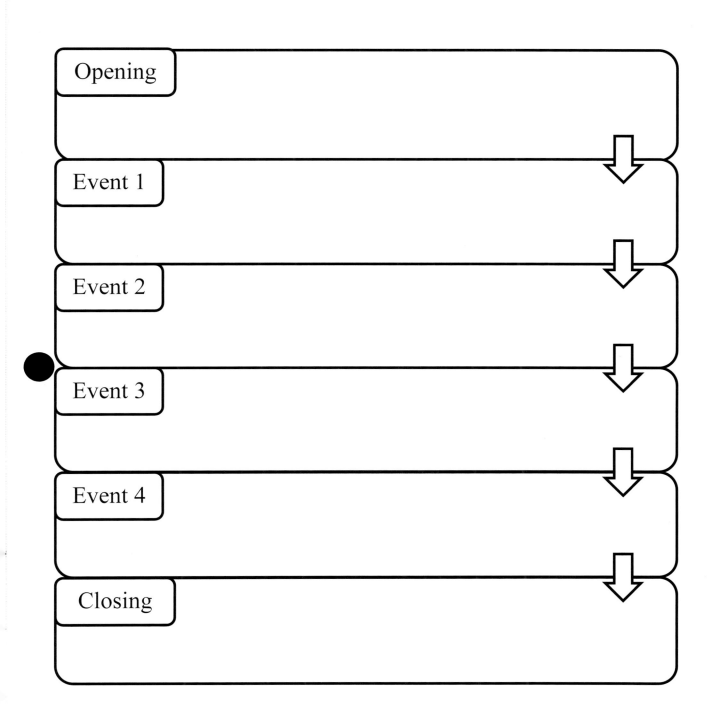

Opening

Event 1

Event 2

Event 3

Event 4

Closing

Imaginative Narrative Checklist

I indented my opening sentence. ___ / 1

My opening sentence grabs my reader's attention. ___ / 1

I wrote at least four events. ___ / 1

I used at least three transitions. ___ / 1

I stayed on topic. ___ / 1

I wrote a closing sentence. ___ / 1

I choke checked my spelling. ___ / 1

Each proper noun and sentence begins with a capital letter. ___ / 1

Each sentence has the correct end mark. . ! ? ___ / 1

My handwriting is neat, and my words are spaced correctly. ___ / 1

Remember, good writing takes practice!

Total Points: ___ / 10

Supplemental Words Levels 1-3

Level 1 Word List - Lesson 9
Words to Begin a Sentence

the	I	a	an	my
it	his	we	he	she
this	her	they	that	(a name)

Level 1 Word List - Lesson 10
Question Words

is	are	do	did
does	can	how	what
when	where	why	who
whom			

Words to Use Instead of...Said

asked	called	stated
cried	demanded	exclaimed
shouted	whispered	replied
remarked		

Words to Use Instead of...Went

ran	rode	walked	crept
drove	biked	tiptoed	hiked
hopped	jumped	jogged	wandered
flew	climbed	strolled	

Words to Use Instead of...Like

love	adore	admire
prefer	care for	enjoy
treasure	favor	appreciate

Supplemental Words Levels 1-3

Words to Use Instead of...Good

great	excellent	marvelous	superior
wonderful	fantastic	splendid	superb
awesome	terrific	stupendous	
grand	extraordinary	amazing	

Words to Use Instead of...Bad

terrible	crummy	awful	lousy
rough	rotten	gross	nasty
dreadful	unpleasant	unfortunate	vile
evil	wicked	despicable	

Words to Use Instead of...Big

large	huge	giant
ginormous	gigantic	immense
tremendous	colossal	massive
jumbo	monster	

Words to Use Instead of...Small

little	tiny	teeny	teensy
short	baby	mini	miniature
	puny	wee	

Words to Use Instead of...Happy

glad	merry	jolly
cheerful	joyful	gleeful
overjoyed	thrilled	pleased
tickled	jubilant	

Supplemental Words Levels 1-3

Words to Use Instead of...Sad

upset   discouraged   troubled   gloomy
disturbed   unhappy   disappointed   down
hopeless   sorrowful   miserable

Words to Use Instead of...Nice

kind   thoughtful   kindly   fair
gracious   pleasant   sweet   charming
agreeable   good   delightful
considerate   lovely

Words to Use Instead of...Pretty

cute   beautiful   handsome   lovely
fair   attractive   stunning   nice
fine   good-looking   glamorous   neat
darling   elegant

Words to Use Instead of...Fast

quick   speedy   nimble   flying
swift   rapid   hasty   snappy
racing   dashing

Words to Use Instead of...Funny

comical   hilarious   ludicrous   ridiculous
playful   humorous   amusing   hysterical
jolly   silly   absurd   entertaining   laughable

Words to Use Instead of...Saw

spied   noticed   observed
noted   sighted   looked(at)
spotted   viewed   perceived

Supplemental Words Levels 1-3

Level 1 Word List - Lesson 22
Colors

red	blue	yellow	green
orange	purple	pink	brown
	black	white	gray

Animals
Level 1 Word List - Lesson 29
Pets

dog	tarantula	gerbil
hamster	frog	mouse
bird	rabbit	fish
snake	lizard	turtle
guinea pig	cat	hermit crab

Animals
Level 1 Word List - Lesson 29
Farm Animals

pig	horse	mule
donkey	goat	sheep	chicken
cow	turkey	duck	goose	rabbit

Onomatopoeia Words

Words that sound like the objects they name or the sounds those objects make.

Onomatopoeia Words

boom	crunch	whoosh	crash	pop
hiss	bzzz	oink	moo	ribbit
quack	woof	splash	swish	slurp
glug	boink	clank	achoo	snip
zing	rip	zip	pow	ding dong
tick tock	eek	whee	crack	vroom

Favorite Things (General Topics)

tv show   toy   book   game   movie

holiday   job   pet   collection   song

season   friend   animal   place

sport   hobby   food   color

activity/thing to do   vacation

Family

parent   child   children   mom   mother

dad   father   sister   brother   son

daughter   aunt   uncle   cousin

grandmother   grandfather

Food

breakfast   cereal   lunch

dinner   dessert   snack

sandwich   drink   candy

ice cream   fruit   vegetable

pizza

Sports

roller skating   softball   baseball

gymnastics   football   bowling

golf   basketball   hockey   swimming

tennis   volleyball   soccer   tee-ball

Assessment Answer Key

Unit One: Assessment Answer Key

Assessment 1 – Letters, Words & Sentences; Spacing Words; and Capitalizing Sentences (Lessons 2-4)
A. Rewrite the following sentences with *spaces* between words.
1. The bed is old.
2. Sam can sing.
3. Dogs are fuzzy.

B. Rewrite each sentence below and *capitalize* the first word.
1. Kat jumps.
2. The fox rests.
3. I jumped in the water.
4. The tram stops.

Assessment 2 – Sentence Subjects and Sentence Predicates (Lessons 5-6)
A. Underline the *subject* of each sentence.
1. The child sang a song.
2. The panda snacks on the twigs.
3. Sal picked the bud.
4. Mom went to the pond.

B. Underline the *predicate* of each sentence.
1. The bunny hopped.
2. Cal tosses the ball.
3. The girl ran up the hill.
4. The frog jumped in the pond.

C. Fill in each blank with one of the following *subjects*.
1. *The truck* sped up the path.
2. *My sister* sang a song.
3. *The small kitten* lapped the milk.

D. Fill in each blank with one of the following *predicates*.
1. The dog *sniffs*.
2. My brother *is Ted*.
3. The fish *has fins*.

E. Complete each sentence with a *subject* or a *predicate*.
Answers may vary.
1. A puppy *licks the boy*.
2. *Sam* called his dad.
3. The robber *hid*.
4. *The girl* bangs the drums.
5. *Mal* washes the truck.

F. Underline the *subjects* and circle the *predicates* in the following sentences.
1. The vet {helped the pet}.
2. The red robin {sang}.
3. Jon {kicks the ball}.
4. I {lost a penny}.
5. The woman {walked to the hill}.

G. Complete the sentences with a *subject* or a *predicate*.
Answers may vary.
1. *The man* ran back.
2. The black cat *slept*.
3. *Seth* dropped his hat.
4. The small kid *jumped*.

Assessment 3 – Complete and Incomplete Sentences (Lessons 7-8)
A. Rewrite the *incomplete sentences* and change them into *complete sentences* on the lines provided.
Answers may vary.
1. The tall girl ran.
2. The puppy ran fast.
3. My brother went to the path.
4. The fuzzy duck waddles.

B. The sentences below are *incomplete*. Write "S" if the sentences are missing a *subject* and "P" if they are missing a *predicate*.
1. P
2. S
3. P
4. P
5. S

C. Finish the *incomplete sentences* on the lines below.
Answers may vary.
1. The big dog runs to me.
2. The duck sat on a log.
3. Jen and Kim swim.
4. Sal went to bed.

Assessment 4 – Declarative, Interrogative, Exclamatory, and Imperative Sentences (Lessons 9-12)
A. Rewrite the *declarative sentence* below so it ends with a period.
Pandas are big.

B. On the line below, write a *declarative sentence*.
Answers may vary.
The robin is red.

C. Rewrite the *interrogative sentence* below so it ends with a question mark.
Are you from Kansas?

D. On the line below, write an *interrogative sentence*.
Answers may vary.
What is the plan?

E. Rewrite the *exclamatory sentence* below so it ends with an exclamation point.
My sister is the best!

F. On the line below, write an *exclamatory sentence*.
Answers may vary.
I like bugs!

G. Rewrite the *imperative sentence* so it ends with a period or exclamation point.
Wash the glass.
OR
Wash the glass!

H. On the line below, write an *imperative sentence*.
Answers may vary.
Walk the dog.
OR
Walk the dog!

Assessment 5 – Practice Writing Sentences (Lesson 13)
A. Write whether each sentence is *declarative*, *interrogative*, *exclamatory*, or *imperative*.
1. Interrogative
2. Declarative
3. Imperative
4. Exclamatory

B. Write sentences according the instructions below.
Answers may vary.
1. Wash the dog.
2. The truck is big!
3. The dress is gold.
4. Is this your hat?

C. The sentences below have mistakes in capitalization and punctuation. Rewrite the sentences correctly.
1. The man went to Texas.
2. Where is my sister?

Assessment 6 – Common and Proper Nouns (Lessons 14-16)
A. Underline all *common nouns* in the sentences below.
1. The fox digs a den.
2. The boy held the box.
3. The man dropped the letter.
4. The bunny sniffed the grass.
5. The woman runs.

B. Underline all the *proper nouns* in the sentences below.
1. Beck hid the lock.
2. Dan went to Kansas.
3. Ben and Pat are brothers.
4. Sid bangs the drums.
5. Mal went to Alaska.

C. Underline all *nouns* in the sentences below.
1. Lin talks to Ken.
2. The boys went to class.
3. Sid swims in the pond.
4. Jon walks on the path.
5. Pandas live in China.

Assessment 7 – Singular and Plural Nouns (Lesson 17)
A. Underline all *singular nouns* in the sentences below.
1. The boy is small.
2. Grab a pen!
3. The woman is tall.
4. Put away the toys.
5. A panda is black and white.

B. Underline all *plural nouns* in the sentences below.
1. Meg kissed her dolls.
2. Grandpa has three cars.
3. The mats are green.
4. The bags are full.
5. A tree is big.

C. Fill in the blank with the *plural* of the indicated noun.
1. Fran saw *cats* at the mall.
2. The *girls* were on a sled.
3. Mom got two *rugs*.
4. The *boxes* fell down the steps!

Assessment 8 – Adjectives (Lesson 18)
A. Underline each *adjective* in the sentences below.
1. I strummed the sad song.
2. Jeb has black shoes.
3. The woman jumped in the cold water.

B. Complete each sentence below with your own *adjective*.
Answers may vary.
1. Tim picked the *pink* candy.
2. Willa had a *new* belt.
3. The *silly* boy hopped.
4. Cam has a *tall* brother.

D. Rewrite each sentence and add your own *adjective*.
Answers may vary.
1. Claire walked to the old bench.
2. The small dog sniffed.
3. The man washes the old truck.
4. The fluffy rabbit hops.
5. The blue glass fell.

Assessment 9 – Action Verbs (Lesson 19)
A. Underline each *action verb* in the sentences below.
1. Jen lifts the box.
2. The buck drinks.
3. The man drops the dish.
4. Liv dances.
5. Ash swims.

B. Complete each sentence below with your own *action verb*.
Answers may vary.
1. The rabbit *hops*.
2. Will *plays* in the attic.
3. The rat *eats* the apple.
4. The girl *runs* to the hill.

C. Fill in each blank with the correct *action verb*.
1. The fish *swims* in the pond.
2. The puppy *sniffs* the boy.
3. Ted *kicked* the soccer ball.
4. The kids *run* by the fence.

Assessment 10 – Nouns, Adjectives, and Action Verbs (Lesson 20)
A. Find and underline the *nouns*, circle the *adjectives*, and draw a box around the *action verbs* in each line below.
1. cat [jump] Jen vest
2. [sang] bird [swim] {hot}
3. child [ran] Kansas {happy}
4. {pink} desk {glad} [said]
5. box {fluffy} [tell] [sit]
6. [called] pug {red} panda
7. belt {odd} [tells] {soft}
8. [gives] Ann {tall} [picked]
9. rabbit [ended] India {cold}
10. {old} woman {long} [sniffs]

Unit One Comprehensive Assessment (Lessons 2-20)
A. Circle the letter next to the correct answer.
1. B
2. D
3. B
4. A
5. B
6. C
7. B
8. B
9. B
10. D

Unit Two: Assessment Answer Key
Teachers, for each composition, students should include each part of the appropriate composition. Use the checklists in the resource section of the Assessment/Resource Booklet for scoring. Use the same composition for the appropriate lesson in the textbook answer key as a guide.

Assessment 11 – Lists of Items & Paragraphs (Lessons 22-31)
A. Circle the letter next to the correct answer.
1. C
2. C
3. B
4. A

Assessment 12 – Personal Letter (Lessons 32-34)
A. Read the *letter* below and label its parts in the correct boxes.
1. Date
2. Greeting
3. Body
4. Closing
5. Signature

B. Write the correct *dates* on the lines provided below. Remember to write the month, day, year, and a comma.
Answers may vary.
1. April 20, 2018
2. April 19, 2018
3. April 21, 2018
4. April 22, 2018
5. December 25, 2018

ASSESSMENT ANSWER KEY

Assessment 13 – Personal Narrative (Lessons 35-38)
A. The events below are not in *order*. Number the events in the
***order* that they happened. Pay attention to *transitions*.**
1. 2, 3, 1
2. 5, 1, 3, 2, 4
3. 1, 3, 2
4. 2, 1, 4, 3, 5
5. 4, 3, 1, 5, 2

Assessment 14 – Imaginative Narrative (Lessons 39-42)
A. The events below are not in *order*. Number the events in the *order*
that they happened. Pay attention to *transitions*.
1. 2, 1, 3
2. 3, 2, 1
3. 5, 1, 3, 2, 4
4. 1, 3, 2
5. 1, 2, 5, 3, 4

Unit Two Comprehensive Assessment (Lessons 22-42)
A. Circle the letter next to the correct answer.
1. C
2. D
3. B
4. A
5. C
6. B
7. A
8. B
9. D
10. B